# A ROGERIAN PERSON-CENTRED APPROACH IN POETRY

# A psychotherapy? No… A lifetime…

Edited by Madeline Bosio

# Dedication

<br>

JUNE 1989

TO YOU MY FRIEND IN HOSPITAL
I said to you: Hold on to the other end
of the red string and pull hard
until you to feel your substance.
I know about your fear of getting lost forever.
It's immense, and when it speaks
one really disappears
if there is no one there who knows the way
for having walked it slowly.
But am not able to tell you
how to live the moment
and remember, at least something,
and together plan.
I still need long absences;
I think it's this, that is saving my life.
Maybe all our struggle
is a powerful request
for respect and for righteous silence…

# Contents

*Don't walk in front of me*
*I may not follow*
*Don't walk behind me*
*I may not lead*
*Just walk beside me*
*and be my friend*

# Introduction by the author

Sometimes the therapeutic journey brings forth a strong need to "fix" the most touching and significant stages of the process It can happen that the person discovers a poetic vein in speaking and narrating.

In fact, moods often find their best expression only through the language and rhythm of poetry.

Thus was a client able to track a pathway, to write a story of sorrow and of memories, pleasant and unpleasant; of the therapeutic process brought forth in her memory, slowly, step by step. Equally slowly she shaped the emerging figures in the fog with the aid of her psychotherapist.

The poems dating from the beginning of the healing process and handed over to me, are the evidence of how long and slow is the "discarding work" of what has been; how difficult it is to abandon defenses that were set up in order to protect oneself from suffering.

Each poem testifies how difficult it is to recall the past, to contact one's emotions and anguish, both experienced and repressed, until their sense is found by means of a crude, maybe cruel rereading of reality. As if we have many pieces of a jigsaw puzzle for which we have lost the picture.

Some verses tell us how hard it is to relinquish illusions and dreams obstinately cultivated in the attempt to realize them; and they show how bitter is this passage through the narrow door of the recognition of the "limits", of the boundaries, in other words, of one's destiny.

At this point of the therapeutic process, animated with a new wisdom, we recover the dialogue, interrupted years ago, with those parts of the "inner child" that have been wandering the world, looking for someone to take care of them.

This wandering around the world, as vain as it is desperate, is due to the permanence of these infantile parts. The adult part is not looking at the world with adult eyes capable of seeing things according to the critical principle of reality and be able to stop searching/craving for someone and to self-govern those parts.

Eventually the "child" shall find peace thanks to the caring that the "adult", now free of the past chains, shall be able to give. The adult will become the child's "caregiver".

The proposal accompanying the presentation of these poems is to share the experience of a therapeutic process.

This essay shall lead the reader into the secrets of a therapy that turns out to be the search for the "true" story of childhood of each one of us. Just as it was experienced by the client, whereas the therapist helps the client to find those parts of the self that were once set aside, that were causing painful feelings that were too unbearable for the child's ego.

After many years of therapeutic work, I have only one desire: to paint, one day, a picture of all those "found again children" who have "recovered" from the phantoms of the past, to look at them walking in many rows, hand in hand, with their eyes still wet with the last tears of their history now solved... With their faces still tired from the wandering of a lifetime, with the innocent hope of "receiving" what they had the right to expect. Eyes of children finally COMPENSATED by their true reality, put in its right place; compensated because they found, at long last, someone who listens to them, believes them, protects them, loves them, takes care of them. Compensated by the adult part that, having found its dignity, now walks in the world sustained by its own legs. This means "being autonomous" or, in other words, having cut the "silver threads" that kept them tied to someone else and to whom they were hanging on in a relationship of dependency and in vain expectation of "their strawberry ice- cream"...

There is no story without sorrow
There is no sorrow without a story
Follow the river that flows in you
Look, listen, feel, live
Unto the sea of pain
Of your child.

*What can one say, how can one explain in words what you "doc" have described in such a profound manner?*

*What can one say to a patient, when with your words, your countenance, your posture you can reach the deepest recesses of one's soul?*

*If only I could describe what I feel! …But I cannot!*

*People like you have an instant ability to transform the dimension, the life, the experience of one's suffering, turning them into support for the other person, along with an inborn generosity and skill acquired over time and also a delicacy, giving the sensation of the absence of a blaming condemnation; comprehension and judgement without bias; and a battle for a "repair" that we children have the right to be given.*

*One is astonished and hopeful reading your words!*

*Your analysis of the person is the perfect description of a painting that, with a brush, is able to create shades of colours on a picture threadbare and old that only an eye and a worn-out soul can capture and make you reflect with a heart-rending cry.*

*One comes to realize, reading the comments on the poems, how cruel is the attempt to modify the child's actualizing tendency.*

*How harmful is the attempt to deprive the child of the freedom to speak out and to find strength in being honest.*

*I am in a muddy and murky marsh. Perhaps some way not to be sucked down by the dense quick-sands does exist. You are on your own: the more you struggle, the more you react, the more you sink.*

*Look! There is a hand above me, I can see it, I lightly touch it, it is offering me a chance to save myself, it's there!*

*Your own hand, you cannot recognize, bears the calluses of the struggle. Worn out by fatigue, and so weak you don't know where to stretch it; almost a stranger to your body.*

*Tenderly, the other hand first holds one finger, then two, then three, then your whole hand, leading you towards your "self." And once you have reached it, it shall let go its hold, because now, maybe, you shall be able to walk alone and hold on to yourself: ot to dreams, and not to others.*

*And like a bird you shall take flight. Flying away from the abyss where a long time ago you yourself fell, exhausted by the pain and the fear to be hurt.*

*Fly little child, fly!*

# Technical Introduction
# What is psychotherapy?
# A new proposal in the form of poetry

Those who work in the field of psychotherapy following a phenomenological-existential approach, identifying with existential philosophy, shall appreciate this new book. In line with philosophical and scientific methodology, the therapeutic journey winds across a succession of emotions and feelings. This kind of therapy cannot be described in prose in accordance with a positivistic matrix because the "client" uses the immediacy of "experiencing"; thus, "sharing" her experience.

Maslow champions "experience" as an essential technique/instrument in psychotherapy, with its roots in existential philosophy. The sharing of one's "experience" is also the pathway of professional growth and penetrating research.

In this essay, Madeline Bosio uses poetry, written by a client during the years of her psychotherapy, finding them to be the perfect means for capturing the process of growth and of changing feelings and emotions along the pathway of the therapy. They are poems that hold the breath of life, the touch of existence, the burden of pain.

This is a story lived out in its crude reality and deep sadness. It is a story of sorrow re-evoked in the Experience of the present; of the here and now that carries within itself, like a geological sample, every element of her personal story. Nothing is lost, everything remains; as in the nucleus of a black hole... all the atoms of the time we lived.

The therapeutic challenge consists in having the capacity to heal the wounds caused by events experienced with suffering, powerlessness, hopelessness and fear and, in particular other situations, with confusion; and in helping the client come to terms with needs that were ignored, and resulting voids. Alongside every poetic voice there is an explanation underlining the historical step taken along the pathway of the psychotherapy.

This is not an essay to read, rather the sharing of an experience, which is the only true path to knowledge. If the experience belongs to the client, then the therapist has no power but to listen; the road "traced" belongs to "Angelina".

Deborah Turchetto
Gynaecologist, psychotherapist

# Preface



This work cannot be and does not aspire to be scientific, since it lacks the scientific basis to be considered as such.

The work has its focus in the area of human experience. The principle is to give a voice to clients and to therapists providing, material of direct clinical experience. It can have validity for naturalistic studies of psychotherapy.

Its experiential contents can make of it a "psychological essay".

Its contents are the therapeutic experience of a client of mine. This client's journey exemplifies the experience I have been able to verify many times in my work as a Rogerian therapist.

While psychoanalysis is an elaboration of the emerging contents through the reality of a "libido", Person- Centered Therapy relies on the pathway and on the experiential "world" of the person and on the history of "that" person.

H. Maslow states in his book *Towards a psychology of Being*, that the best way to comprehend the human being, or at least a way that is necessary in certain circumstances, is to enter his *Weltanschauung* that is "his way of life," so as to be able to see "his" world through "his eyes". This is the Rogerian "frame of reference"...

Such a conclusion is "poles" apart from any scientific positivistic philosophy or research. Naturalistic research seeks to describe and understand phenomena in naturally occurring settings.

Angelina's psychotherapy is an intervention according to the techniques of the Rogerian school of thought.

The work confirms that psychotherapy can effect change and that emotions and feelings play a very important role in giving rise to changes.

This work also confirms Maslow's "theory of needs" and the concepts of existential philosophy; concepts and theories that were confirmed by Carl Rogers.

The "way of being" achieved by the client who follows all the steps towards the restoration of a "true" self, is existential.

The concepts I am voicing, are the outcome of a "natural" evolution of my non-directive work, used in the interaction with the client.

At the end of the journey of a "therapy of compensation," as Maslow calls it, "becoming" is integrated and interacts with "being". This corresponds to Rogers' being in the "here and now" in harmony with one's actualizing tendency.

Potentialities are fully realized, the inner world is free to voice itself without being distorted, repressed or denied.

Other concepts concerning the "therapeutic process" are an elaboration theorized by me. It has evolved through my personal experience in my professional work.

In my opinion, when therapy goes down to the deepest roots of experience, a deadly fear appears.

The fear that prevents the child from coping with "reality" not only because of its age, when there is very little trust, very little sense of worth, where the "grass" of dignity is only trying to "peep up", but also, and especially, because of having to deal with careless or violent caregivers.

In this frame of reference it is impossible for the child to face or cope with "reality".

"Fear" accompanies the experience of the feeling of being "alone" in those moments when the child "instinctively" feels a need for and seeks protection and unconditional love and positive regard...

Impotence works the final act of feeling and experiencing being "ALONE"... Alone without any help and at the mercy of the world outside...

I take the liberty of pointing out these concepts supported by Maslow's words concerning the benefit of the experience of those working in the psychotherapeutic field and who recognize themselves in existential philosophy, in order to foster a research in this direction.

Maslow mentions the need to start from an "experiential knowledge" rather than through conceptual systems or abstract categories.

Existentialism has its roots in phenomenology in that it uses the personal subjective experience as the foundation from which abstract knowledge derives.

Rogers says: *"it is the client who knows what hurts, what directions to go, which problems are crucial, which experiences have been deeply buried".* (original quotation from On Becoming a Person).

The best attitude is to entrust the client with understanding the right direction in the therapeutic process. (Rogers, 1967)

Some of my concepts have very simple names. They are the words I have used and still use with my clients (such as "silver threads" or "strawberry ice cream"), experiencing the deep emotional and intellectual effect they have on the client.

My work is in response to Maslow's request to verify his theory.

His "theory of needs" is broadly confirmed.

The same regards other concepts:

The "theory of compensation" is widely evident in several poems written by Angelina.

Malaise is caused by a "way of being" made up of a distorted self, reiterations, "historical pains" that do not allow the person to "function as a whole"...

All of these concepts are widely confirmed by Rogers.

The therapeutic "challenge" consists in:

- Being able to heal the wounds from experiences that caused pain, fear and impotence, and sometimes also confusion in children having to deal with highly disturbed adults;

- Coming to terms with the unmet needs and the consequential "voids".

The most delicate, if not the most difficult work consists in integrating the "inner child" with the adult.

The "circle" is closed, that is, the two ends join together when the original emotions linked to specific "pieces" of the "puzzle of reality" belonging to the experiences of childhood, are "re-covered", thus, recognized and accepted; given citizenship, as Rogers says.

The last act is "the funeral" of my dreams, built upon my wounds and voids.

At this point, the pieces of the puzzle are back in their rightful places. This is how "beginning" and "end" come together, and the circle is closed. In other words, when beginning and end "come to terms".

The ancient feelings, that once had been concealed or removed, but nonetheless "had been operating" in distorted manners, shall give way to the feelings of trust, worth and self- esteem now gained by the adult.

It is the "way of being" the child would have developed had he had the parents described by Maslow: growing according to ones actualizing tendency.

Maslow states that changes are not the result of acquiring new habits or associations, but rather derive from the integration of "parts" of the self. Integration follows a careful process of "shedding" defensive mechanisms adopted that were to conceal those wounds and pains so unbearable for the self, as well as other behavioural patterns used as futile strategies to satisfy our needs. Personal Power appears in all its authenticity.

Maslow clearly states that the behaviour of a self-realized person is "created" and freed released rather than acquired. This is what Rogers calls the: "Actualizing tendency".

# The poems

This collection of poems is the journey of a client whom I shall name Angelina, but it could be the journey of many other Angelina or Angelino; all those who re-walk the pathway of their life story.

The therapeutic process becomes a complete "work of art" when, besides the integration of all the parts of the self, there is a change in behavioural patterns used in the attempt to avoid anxiety, anguish, fear, confusion and reality; in the strategies aimed at satisfying our primary needs.

As Carl Rogers writes:

"Mankind has no limits as regards potentialities Once authentic dialogue has been restored, human beings are in an endless process of "becoming", the actualizing tendency is timeless.

The actualizing tendency is a characteristic of organic life, of which the human organism is one aspect. There is also, beyond this, a "formative tendency" that also characterises the universe as a whole. (C. Rogers 1980 *A way of being*).

These poems represent a small part of the therapeutic process, following the client's stream of life.

Thank you to Angelina and to all the Angelinas and Angelinos I have met walking side by side with them throughout the therapeutic process, whether it was lengthy or brief

Their stories and their pathways have been a precious contribution to my work and my personal growth.

Special thanks go to Angela Romito, a lawyer who defends and protects children's rights.

Her sensitivity superb and the work she carries out are

recognizable in the solemn tone colouring her words in the following introduction.

"Thank you, Angie…"

Dreams are like that "strawberry ice cream" that is our "VITAL" request: the ancestral longing/hunger. this need has remained, because it was not attended to by him/her who was naturally supposed to satisfy it, then it shall be our company, step after step in the years to come, a "faithful and bastard tyrant".

An "introduction worthy of respect" should bear the gift of clarity in the attempt to lead the reader to better understanding the arcane mystery hidden in the verses of the poetry.

Well… This is not an "introduction worthy of due respect"…

One cannot explain, nor can one understand, and it is only a chimera, that of a client – Angelina – who is the psychotherapy itself.

Well, then what can we do? Desist, me from writing, you from reading?

Maybe it would be easier and surely it should be less "troublesome"… However, we cannot, neither I nor you.

Our search is an arduous task that winds around a skein of "silver threads" that we carry with us and wrap around him or her whom we have "chosen to satisfy our frustrated needs". Life, then, shall manage to turn those unsatisfied needs into "dreams" that, more or less unconsciously, invest in others.

A slow maturity, a "tank" of trust and a "caravan" of love for ourselves – that is, self-acceptance – shall help us in the inescapable reading of past and present reality leading us towards the processing of much "hidden grief" and the healing of wounds suffered, giving us, later, the strength to "take part in the many funerals" of our dreams/frustrated needs; and to fill the voids with void.

You know very well the pain that flows like life-blood in the folds of your broken limbs. I, like you.

To you are not concealed endless successions of losses, achievements, hopes, defenses, failures that, just like the growth rings visible of the trunk of an oak tree can mark the plane age, in the same way they also mark your "age" and mine.

So... The point is not to give up that strawberry ice-cream to the point of erasing its image, colour, and taste; nor is it to replace it with a different ice-cream or some other surrogate. We must only stop asking it of those who cannot or do not want to give it to us; of those who never had it or who want to keep it for themselves. We must accept reality just as it was, and accept that it can never  has been and that it can never be changed.

Reality that mat have been crude and, for some, also cruel.

Duels, battles and wars are only against ourselves. "Defeat" carries with it a melancholy SELF, regret for what "I could have had"... "Surrender" implies separation, the courage to say "farewell", to say farewell to oneself; it is the fruit of a crisis and thus of a choice.

The poems simply testify to the same "stripping" of defenses set up like walls protecting from suffering. Each verse is a piece of a mosaic that is finally completed, allowing us to dialogue with our inner child, who for years "wandered the world, a "restless acrobat" looking for someone who simply wanted her just as  she was, only to find "that someone" in her own adult part. The liberated adult can now, at last,  for it wanted nothing else, take care of the inner child, hugging and caressing her and covering her with kisses.

Psychotherapy is the necessary journey of a childhood that wants, or better still, is allowed to surface from the meanderings of the subconscious world. The therapist is the essential friend who helps to find those fragments that long ago were banished to the deepest recesses of our inner child, for they bore unbearable sorrows...

# Lost

The strength to stand up and move with the burden of her sorrow; with the distressing anguish of knowing to be alone, is a HOWL OF PAIN.

# Lost

My first steps in
my solitude.
Bitter is existence
bitter is expectation
empty remains the stretched hand.
What are you waiting for? A crumb of love.
Bitter is the morsel begged for and given.
Can't exist in the non-existent.
But I don't know my decision.
One must die to be reborn.
Languish is only dying a little..
Oh! It's not fair, I don't want to die
I am dying without dying.
Kill me…
I must retrace my steps
of a long way back
and search for what I left
behind. Rediscover. Retrieve.
Examine. Remove and
I will have to rummage and perhaps
gather up only
that is left…

December 1987

# Silence

The pain is soothed, the journey has started. It seems that Angelina is connected with some parts or memories of herself she had forgotten; some are clear, others unsettling and invisible.

# Silence

People swim in water, I
swim in the warm wind that enfolds me
of sunny days.
I swim in the warm light of the sun,
swim in the silence of the warm summer landscape.
No-one is there. A red dusty road
and rugged; straight; in the mirage
of the heat. Yellow sand; bushes
withered and covered with
the dust of silence.
A smell of dry resin and
silence, and no- one. No… there was
someone present, there: Silence. I
feel its presence… it
keeps me company… I and he
…alone… and a long road
burnt by the sun. And even the
waves of heat, to the eyes
of me child, turn into presences,
gentile presence and mysterious…
All around were: scents and
wonder and a fear, slight
and disquieting. A something present:
'twas the INVISIBLE…

June 1988

# Sorrow

Angelina accepts and reclaims the pain of having been unheard and she entrusts herself to her therapist.

# Sorrow

Mother...
It was my pain
        that I wanted to bring to you
It was my pain
        that I wanted to show you
It was my pain
        I wanted to give you
I wanted you to hold it
        in your hands
I wanted you to show me
        that nothing, was there to fear
I wanted you to take it
        for me.

But I had learned
        that you would have allowed me not
But I had learned
        that much I would have risked
and I wandered and wandered and wandered
        until I found where I would have left it...

November 1988

# The wall

Feelings struggle to express themselves owing to the barrier built up over the time. Angelina has a clear sense of the wall and of the difficulty of "dissolving" it... And it becomes a dialogue with melancholy.

# The wall

There is a wall…
my emotions are flowing, slipping
along a hard- bedded river
"I never heard you;
silent and infinite presence
of my life
*You finally heard me*
Your name is melancholy, isn't it?
*Yes; it's a long time I have been waiting. A lifetime.*
Your face I recognized
but I never liked it.
*For years I have been here. For years lonely am I,*
*I do not see. I do not hear. But your presence I feel.*
*Take me, heal me, cuddle me,*
*do not leave me, I don't know where to go*
*because I do not know how to walk*
But who are you? Why do you exist?
Where do you come from?
How did you come?
*I don't know… It's I… melancholy…*
I don't know how to live…
What can I do for you?
*I don't know, stay with me*
*Wait for me.*
*Your wall, the closed doors*
*have been my life…*
I am tired… you know… of feeling a stranger to myself…
But you melancholy,… who are you?!…

September 1989

# Duels

Angelina tries to react in her present world, but she meets obstacles and reinforced manoeuvers against her. Yet she also understands, though unable to change anything, how self-defeating are her behaviours.

# Duels

I am tired – my heart does not breathe – I feel its beating
it reaches up to my throat – I am grasping –
every dialogue is a duel; every dialogue is an attack
I have come to see that, to all I must obey;
to all I must explain –
to all I offer myself... and here... I get confused...
My availability has become everything – and for everyone –
but it didn't teach me to defend myself...
I have always justified myself, I have always explained...
It didn't teach me to keep a distance...
to say "no" for me
to keep "space" for me
it didn't teach me to "preserve" myself
but I have always accepted attacks; unable to react.
Explained, explained, explained,
trying to change others' intentions...
So they would "leave me be"...
Instead of "finding" I, myself, the way
to be "left in peace", by saying "no",
not being always available,
ready for use... ready when needed...
 offering myself in sacrifice – in strain –
ever me the one to curtail – to change my things
so as to "accommodate" the other's needs...

October 1989

# Never more

The battle between a reality that is clearly a failure in terms of her experience and the "dream" that cannot and must not disappear.

# Never more

I no longer expect anything more
Because I have discovered that
nobody was waiting for me
and that nobody shall ever wait
if they have decide
not to do so…
they are unreachable…
mother
how long did I wait for you
but you weren't there…
but you don't see me
because elsewhere you are facing.
How long I deceived myself:
"there you are… yes… this time!…
and then this! …and then…"
and then NEVER…

November 1989

# My reality

Having accepted, partly, the futility of the struggle for loving consideration, Angelina can clearly see "the games" being played on the other side.

# My reality

How many times did I ask you to look at reality
So many times you replied that I was raving
How many times did I check over and over again, for fear
I was mistaken. But just as many times
reality turned out to be the same again... "it fit"... but...
you...
Those times we both came up against
the same reality, you asked me the favour
of concealing it and I, ready, and I, hungry for love,
would comply with you, because "yes, this time"
you had seen me; we would be together...
at last... I had conquered "that" place inside you.
But when I would ask you: "Do you remember that time?"
"Do you remember that thing? Remember how it turned
out?" You
would reply: "What thing?... WHAT?...
You are raving!!..."
You had planned it all only for yourself
In order to tidy away your not seeing
And once again I discover that you weren't there... you had
Never been there ... you would never be...
that you did not see me... that you have never seen me...
that you shall never see me... because... THE REALITY
IS...
that I DON'T EXIST for you!!...

March 1990

# A blade of grass

The contact with her inner void leads Angelina to nothingness and the limits of "existing".

Once we have come to terms with our: Inner void, we must deal with the Exterior sense of nothingness and the "non-sense" of existing, from the existential/philosophical point of view…

Reality or Emptiness, is not a state of nothingness, but the very source of life , the essence of things. The freedom that leads to Cosmic Love.

# A blade of grass

A blade of grass
and Nothingness... are Nothing
A silence and
Inertia... are Nothing
Nothing can be something.
Something doesn't exist, because:
Nothing and the absolute are the same thing
To be or not to be in this dimension
are the same thing.
Here and there, they are equivalent...

November 1990

# Farewell

The games played by the parent are now made clear, as are the consequences suffered from playing in others' games. Clearer, too, is the arduous path Angelina has followed, in order to gain autonomy and begin to love and respect herself.

# Farewell

Mother,
Why did you choose me for your deadly games?
I feel ill,
the negative vomiting of death rising.
You struck me dead
When you decided my fate.
I have never been able to think
that I could also steal
that I could also not study
that I could also be the first to play
that I could also be the first to use the racket.
You crippled me
and I had to crawl
until I was able to love myself
and now it's I
who from the other side of the bank,
say to myself:
Oh! Hey, there is Angelina!!...
Farewell… my sweet enemy…
December 1990

# Forgive me

Angelina discovers that she, too, seeks to deny freedom to those she loves.

# Forgive me

I want to let you be free
I want to let you fly
I want to let you glide
upon the notes of life;
I want to let leave your life
In your hands. Forgive me…
I stole so much from you.

February 1991

# It has been a great act of love

Angelina discovers that both her inner child and the adult within her. have "sold" themselves in a great act of love, hoping to obtain, what she needed.

## It has been a great act of love

Yes, yes, yes ... Yes, yes, anything you want
but do give me... What you don't want to give
but do give me something... Why don't you want to?!
Innocent victim of your troubles
give me what you don't want to give.
But you have not resolved your troubles
but thus you do what you will with me.
Why am I a victim of your games?...

March 1991

# It lies in you…

The therapy has gone beyond the self- research and has briefly explored her mother's childhood, trying to connect inner parts of the mother with "behavioural patterns" in Angelina's family. A painful part of Angelina seems to belong to a part that the mother denied within herself, or with which she has been unable to come to terms. These aspects of the parent can be figured out when we "no longer question question…" We spend our existence trying to understand others. Once we have solved "our problems", we no longer need to understand them, because we now "can see them" (as an Indian philosopher once told me…)

# It lies in you…

Oh! Mummy I looked at you
and there I met myself
Before me stood
my little one when she was ill

She was there, outside of me
but now is in her rightful place
a place that is within you.

I saw you, fragile and unloved
I recognized you and all at once loved you
I shall never forsake you
I shall love you for that love
That you were never able to give to me…
I AM FREE…

April 1992

# Immortality

...When all the "silver threads" have been cut, there remains only you... and the essence of things, stripped or disrobed of all that was built by our needs, by our dreams, by our values... What remains is "being" in its "essentiality".

# Immortality

It is in the silence
of essence that
I calmed myself.
It is in the silence
of essence
that I found
the immortality
of the emotion
for you mother.
An emotion that
now is timeless
stripped of all that has been…

February 1993

# Silences

...Soothed is the pain, soothed the dogged research, soothed all requests... The fog fades away along with the fatigue of being...

# Silences

Silences continue to descend
like stars
they descend over your
chaos and disorders
and anger vanishes
and rancor vanishes
all quietens
I saw that
chaos and disorders
belong to your life
Silence streams down
also on the whys
and doubt fades away
never more shall I trample on
your untilled gardens
they are more sacred
than my silence.

March 1993

# Intruder

Angelina has succeeded in freeing herself from the bonds of dependency with her mother. She no longer asks herself the reason for things. At last she can clearly see her mother with her own problems.

# Intruder

They threw you out of the nest and
the same you did to me.
You would stand looking from a corner
at the favourite, who from those knees
so desired by you,
sent, enemy, sneers at your pain
I, too, for many looked
for warm arms that would afford me
a little love,
a small place in that nest.
A lifetime I spent protecting and decorating
others' nests only to feel like an intruder
To you, too, I offered many things of mine
but you don't want them; they aren't what you want
because you, too, have a
favourite: the one you protected
against me, so she would remain
untouched by me, an enemy
who really was only asking for love.
And now that nests of others
no longer I seek, returns
the original cry:
give me crumbs of love
I too want wings of love…
But the cry fades away
in the certainty that
 the game is over now
and all that remains
is to rise again…
but… where?…

March 1994

# Oh Rocky Rocky

The pain for her dog's death opens a wound and thoughts on mourning and the meaning of life.

# Oh Rocky Rocky

Oh Rocky, Rocky
You left
When least we expected it
I cried so much
of a desperate torment
not because you passed away
but because you are no longer here
it's your existence that
is a great absence
you left a great emptiness
of presence, of games and
of rituals
A void I thought
I never would fill
but it has filled ...
Who knows! ...it can be filled...
when I find a name:
nothingness
You were and no longer
are, never more
you went into the NOTHINGNESS
and this is the last gift you have given me.

June 1994

# Don't smile

Now Angelina must come to terms with her habitual but dysfunctional patterns of behaviours, that her restored dignity now prevents her using. However, it shall take a while. before she can change them…

# Don't smile

Oh please my dear child
don't smile, no don't smile, I pray you
Oh, No! Don't smile anymore my dear child,
I pray to you
No more must you hide, my dear child,
your sorrow, your shame
innocent
behind your beautiful smile.
The Masters of power
are not worthy
of your sweet smile.
Come, I shall take you far away with me
where you shall be able to laugh and laugh
in the wind of freedom
that shan't ever hurt you.

November 1995

# The search

With a gentle whisper "tell me," Angelina embraces or reconstructs all that… MIGHT HAVE BEEN…

# The search

My love... tell me... tell me what you need
Oh yes... the sweet voice that tenderly says:
love, my love, tell me what you want
my love... tell me what can I do for you
I am here for you
I am here... I am listening to you
I am here... I care for you...
Oh yes my love... I am waiting for you...
A dream that in through time,
re-found in this moment... now for myself.

November 1996

# My dear sweet friend

Angelina writes this verse to a young friend, the adolescent; son of a friend she has just visited.

# My dear sweet friend

My dear sweet friend
the pain you are hiding
so as not to suffer the harm
they caused you
and perhaps still are causing you
is mutely howling in the silence
of your drawers.
Do not wait until you separate
entirely from it…
it's what has been saving your life…

December 1996

# Why?

Angelina is struck by the suffering of her young friend and tries to contact with and identify his pain and state of mood. Thus she figures out his sorrow caused by his father.

# Why?

Oh! Why when I speak to you
do I feel my hands
slipping along a smooth wall
without holds?
Why do my words
never arrive inside you?
But I see them slide
along your walls of ice?
But I, victim...
You won't listen to me
You don't hear me
You are deaf and don't see me
You take nothing
of what I offer you
but you have the strength to
throw on me and into me
all your world, cold and
sometimes cruel.
And I am now left
with no cards to play
because I have played them all
in the effort to be heard and understood.
Now I feel myself full of you,
and I am no more.
Where are my words?
Help me!!...
Where are my thoughts
that are not yours?
Nobody wanted them and I lost them.
Perhaps I shall acquire a friend
who found them
and is keeping them for me.
Who are you, friend of mine?

December 1996

# To my father

Angelina closes the "circle" of her search with a... "farewell" to her father.

# To my father

Dear friend of mine
Where were you while
they were bending me to their will?
Your smile without words
your gaze without reproof
your knees, bulwarks against sorrow
saved my life.
Why wouldn't you speak?
Why weren't you my ally?...
Oh!... Maybe it was only the little boy
whom you too were carrying
hidden inside of you
and who helpless saw me
but who, power did not have...
I wish you were still here my friend
so I could now smile at your grumbles...

May 1997

# I can see you... Take courage

Angelina understands she cannot do anything for others if not "being there" with her presence; the presence of a person who no longer seeks to act for or to understand, but only to "be there". Angelina speaks to the courage of her friend as strength to go on and to her courage as the "will" to be and to exist.

# I can see you… Take courage

Impervious walls
Disquieting nights
Bursting cries
Unceasing storms
Come on! Take courage
my friend.
I can see your pathway
I feel the tearing of your wounds
bleeding
there where they lean
on the burning rocks
 so sharp.
Don't turn around for now
to consider your past…
…too stinging
is what you feel…
At last you can cry
and die to your sorrow.
I am here… I am looking at you…
I feel you… I am listening to you…
I would like… would like… would like…
but I can only
listen and look…
at your life that
you too must retrace
in the life cycle
 recalling – dying – and being reborn
to yourself…
A path unnecessary
 had they let you
live of yourself
AND
given only a hand that
answered your call:
- "mummy…"
- "tell me… my love…"
July 1997

# Found again

Angelina gets in touch on an emotional level with the social dimension in which she has developed over the years the need to reverse unbearable situations so as to create stability, balance, justice. An analysis of the present, along with the analysis of the past, enables her to make links with the past and do away with all such links, but also with those set up in the present life with the emotions of before. This brought a change in her emotional reactions and thus also behavioural patterns.

# Found again

What a mess of absurd sounds
how much crossing of black and stormy clouds
how many unexpected freezing showers
how much deaf noise without warning
how much snarling without reason.
It's there where I found you again little Angelina.
After a long path walked
retracing
my steps.
It's there where I left you...since a lifetime.
Hiding you under the blanket of
my desperate attempt to create
harmony...at any cost...
At the cost of your life...of my life
And I who sold myself
to repair messes that were not mine
but that became part of my life.
I returned to take you back
little Angelina
And to take you away
With me
Forever...

April 1999

# April '99

Angelina chooses a date as the title of the poem. Now there are no longer situations to get through, but a life to live, stripped of all that has been before. It took a long time not to be caught out again by illusions and to get rid of all the old patterns. But in the end her love for herself prevailed and she won her battle against illusions, and so she began the true battle, made only of herself.

# April '99

The herons are taking away in flight
they choose a direction...
no a different one... they fly around, they come back...
perhaps they want to stay...
but thence they find the vital urge
and away... away
They rise higher and higher
become more and more small
their claws become threads...
like my pink balloons
the silver thread of which
I let slip away in my hand
and with my dreams they fly away
far away.
Together with the herons
they become small dots far away
        and
they shan't be here
when the herons return
because that flight
is an outbound flight.
And now I can live.

*"You shall take nothing but your memories"*

# Notes

# The Void

*... "void can be filled only with void..."*

Void is the "experience" created by needs left unfulfilled. We try to fill voids with substitutes such as people, things, events, or other surrogates, so as to avoid the pain  and sorrow of the unmet. Sometimes we succeed in getting what we need, but it is never enough. Even though we receive it, there is always a taste of dissatisfaction. This is the "void" that keeps on emitting its cry of sorrow since it cannot recognize "the surrogate".

Why? – Because the present is not the past. "Those cells" can desire, and recognize only what they needed when they needed it in the past.

Only the part of us that is now adult, will be able to "fill" that need/void and it will do so by acknowledging the story of "the void," accepting that the "need" shall never be satisfied and that "void" is an "experience".

# Strawberry ice cream
## Running on empty

A metaphor:

Strawberry ice cream represents "the specific need" of our story: "I need **that** color and **that** taste". In other words: it must be given by **That Person** and in **that** moment (my caregiver). If this does not happen, there is a frustrating experience (The "not-given").

This is extremely important to note the "not-given" is the experience that gives rise to a "void" that colours interactions with others with the aim of filling the void (using the silver threads). There is a specific "way of being": *Selling myself*, says Angelina; and a specific "inner longing": *I need your appreciation*. This request becomes my strawberry ice cream…

Let us put all this in another way so we can clearly understand.

This kind of experience causes wounds and voids that the child first, and the adult later, shall try to fill. That is, they try to satisfy the need unmet using "silver threads", winding them around "the other", in order to "drink the nectar" our caregivers never gave us. This is why it's so difficult to "let go" those threads, to which we are desperately attached.

The "running" is running after the dream.

The "empty" is the void.

# Silver threads

The "silver thread" is the metaphoric representation of the needs/dreams we incessantly strive to realise. We walk "around the world" trying to wind them around others. These threads consist of our needs; and we would like them nurture us.

Unfortunately, the nurturing is "neurotic" in so far as we hope that someone might give us what we did not receive during our childhood.

When I wrote to Angelina for her consent to publish the book, the following is part of the letter she answered.

... I remember the poem: Don't Smile; I always smiled in reaction to my offenders, but also when hoping to "be part" of something having to do with: "Let's be together" – Let's do something together" – Let's be friends, says Bruce Springsteen". Now I am strong and I tried to use that smile in everyday life, but in this world of individualism and grandstanding it didn't work; I understand it needs "conditional regard". Since I no longer need to rely on someone or something; since I am no longer a stranger to myself (Remember my dialogue with melancholy?) I take my little girl with me, hand in hand, and we go on our own. Now I have a reference point of my own, within me; built through self-esteem and trust. I now move with my own steering compass, not given to me by nature, as it is naturally given to the herons of my poem; not given to me with the aid of my caregivers as it would have been natural, but on my own, thanks to you Maddalena. ...

When I read this part, I whispered in the wind: "Yes, I helped you my dear, but you are the one who did all the work.

Thanks to you Angelina."

# Acknowledgements

Thank you to "Angelina" who, over the years, handed me numerous scraps of paper bearing the poems she would write on the train taking her home after our sessions.
Endless thanks to all my clients who gave me, and are still giving me, the opportunity to learn and to grow in wisdom, respect and universal love.

# Read *You shall thank your enemies and love your story*

The book explains and describes the pathways leading to neurotic behaviours, beginning from early years of life, when we set up behavioural patterns that turn out to be fallatious, as regard our needs as well as our interactions with others. There are dreams which are defensive constructions in the name of unsatisfied needs of our childhood; against realities and family dynamics too different and dangerous to cope with, in a developmental stage when a child has no instruments to face or deal with such "troubled waters". Certain fears in adulthood, overwhelming though irrational to intellect, are the outcome of those moments, when a child was unable to face reality, being at the mercy of oneself, impotent, thus in danger and without a protecting caregiver. In this healing process, shared with a psychotherapist, in a long and painful revisitation of what occured, the unveiling of an emotional world silenced long ago, we dismantle paths built with so much struggle. When we plough into the past with the "experiential" model, there will be a change in our way of being and an enrichment in our interactions with others. The book has a second part dealing with sex abuse in childhood and disruptive relationships.

# Read *Short-Circuit and betrayal in child sexual abuse*

The book describes a research in the field of child sex abuse. The intent is to point out specific aspects which will lead to a complete psychological recovery from trauma using the "Experiential Model" and moving back to the roots of the traumatic experience. The fact fostering a "total healing" is the individuation of the uncompleted "existential act", interrupted at the moment of the "molesting act". The specific aspect has to do with a "specific need" in the victim's story. The Rogerian approach is appropriate for the client to get in touch with the world of emotions and *go deep down* to parts of the Self that lead to the "black hole": the root bearing the experience of illusions - betrayal - defeat. At the same time it *leads up to the peak* of compassion and cosmic love. Thence, there, there it's gonna be another *"long walk home"*.